©CreativeCommons 2.0, Bev Syke/wiki commons, Billy Hathorn/wiki commons,
Marco Almbauer/wiki commons, Tony Hisgett/wiki commons, Gladassfanny/Getty
Images, DenisTangneyJr/iStock Images, Alex Maclean/Getty Images, Papa Bravo/
Shutterstock, Coco-rentin/Shutterstock, Radharc Images/Alamy Stock Photo

Published by Sourcebooks Wonderland, an imprint of Sourcebooks Kids
P.O. Box 4410, Naperville, Illinois 60567-4410
(630) 961-3900
sourcebookskids.com

Library of Congress Cataloging-in-Publication Data is on file with the publisher.

Source of Production: 1010 Printing Asia Limited, North Point, Hong Kong, China
Date of Production: May 2019
Run Number: 5014961

Printed and bound in China.
OGP 10 9 8 7 6 5 4 3 2 1

HIDE AND SEEK
BOSTON

BY ERIN GUENDELSBERGER   PICTURES BY MATTIA CERATO

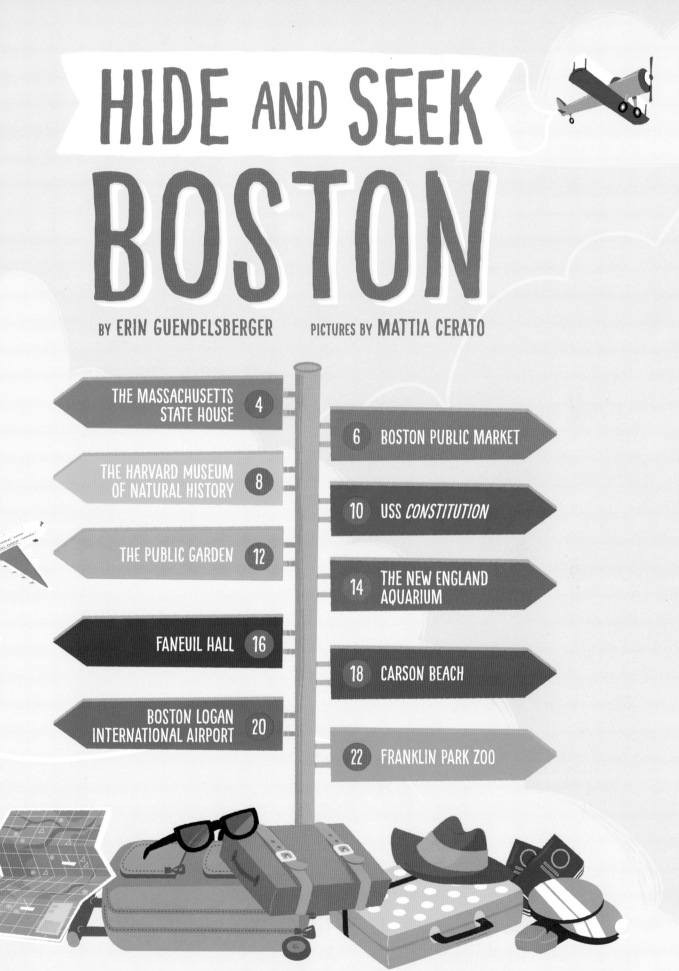

sourcebooks
wonderland

WELCOME TO BOSTON—THE BEST CITY IN THE WORLD!

I'm the mayor of this beautiful city, and I need your help. I'm creating an exhibit to feature the greatest parts of Boston, and I am sending YOU on a quest to find the items that represent these places! This chart has everything you need to keep an eye out for and where you need to look.

PREPARE TO BE AMAZED—YOU'RE ABOUT TO EXPLORE AND LEARN ABOUT SOME OF THE BEST MUSEUMS, PARKS, AND ATTRACTIONS THE WORLD HAS EVER SEEN!

MAYOR

THE MASSACHUSETTS STATE HOUSE

THE MASSACHUSETTS STATE HOUSE, considered one of the most magnificent buildings in the country, was completed on January 11, 1798. The area of land originally belonged to **JOHN HANCOCK**, a Revolutionary War hero and the first elected Massachusetts state governor. The building's distinctive **GILDED DOME** was initially made of wood, but it was covered in copper by Paul Revere's company in 1802 and covered again with **23-KARAT GOLD LEAF** in 1874. The dome was painted gray during WWII to protect the city from possible bomb attacks.

The State House is one of the oldest buildings on **BEACON HILL**, and its grounds include statues of orator Daniel Webster, educator Horace Mann, Civil War General Joseph Hooker, and President John F. Kennedy, among others. The current Massachusetts Senate and House of Representatives still meet here.

CAN YOU FIND...

BOSTON PUBLIC MARKET

The **BOSTON PUBLIC MARKET** is a year-round, indoor marketplace with fresh groceries and agricultural products. The market opened on July 30, 2015, with the goal of providing the community with fresh food and educating the public about nutrition and preparation.

Visitors to the market can buy seasonal food that is produced or originates in **MASSACHUSETTS** and **NEW ENGLAND**, including fresh produce, meat, poultry, eggs, milk, cheese, fish, bread, baked goods, beverages, flowers, and more! The market includes **35 LOCAL FARMERS**, fishers, and food entrepreneurs, as well as short-term "pop-up" vendors. There is also a **3,200-SQUARE-FOOT KITCHEN** where visitors can experience hands-on cooking demonstrations, lectures, family activities, and more.

CAN YOU FIND...

THE HARVARD MUSEUM OF NATURAL HISTORY was established in 1998 to enhance public understanding and appreciation of the natural world and is comprised of three research museums. The **MUSEUM OF COMPARATIVE ZOOLOGY** has more than twenty-one million specimens, and the **HARVARD UNIVERSITY HERBARIA** has more than five million. The **MINERALOGICAL AND GEOLOGICAL MUSEUM** has more than 100,000 mineral specimens, more than 200,000 rock and ore specimens, and large meteorite and gem collections. The mineral collection began in 1784 and is the oldest university mineral collection in the United States.

Each year, more than **250,000 PEOPLE** visit the museum. Visitors can explore exhibits about Africa, Asia, and Central and South America, as well as about New England forests. They can also learn about dinosaurs, bees, birds, mammals, microbial life, marine life, evolution, and climate change.

CAN YOU FIND...

USS CONSTITUTION

The **USS _CONSTITUTION_** is the world's oldest commissioned warship still afloat. Weighing **1,576 TONS** and standing **189 FEET ABOVE WATER** at its tallest point, the ship sits in Boston Harbor. The USS _Constitution_ was first launched in 1797 and completed 58 years of active naval service, **WINNING 33 BATTLES** and losing none. During the War of 1812, the USS _Constitution_ defeated Britain's HMS _Guerriere_ in just thirty-five minutes. When a British cannonball bounced off the _Constitution's_ hull, a British sailor supposedly cried, "Huzzah! Her sides are made of iron!"—hence the ship's nickname, "**OLD IRONSIDES**."

More than **500,000 VISITORS** tour the ship every year and visit the nearby USS Constitution Museum. There is an active crew of sailors dressed in 19th-century naval uniforms stationed on the ship to tell stories and answer questions for visitors!

CAN YOU FIND...

CAN YOU ALSO LOOK FOR THESE THINGS?

THE PUBLIC GARDEN

In 1837, a private association of Bostonians petitioned the city to establish a botanical garden, and in 1838, an area along the Charles River was officially designated as **THE PUBLIC GARDEN**, the first public botanical garden in the U.S. In 1877, **SWAN BOATS** designed by Robert Paget first glided through the lagoon and are still operated by the Paget family today!

The Public Garden includes **24 ACRES** of green space, plants, lagoon, fountains, and monuments. The oldest monument, **THE ETHER FOUNTAIN**, was built in 1868 to honor the discovery of ether and its use in the Massachusetts General Hospital. The second monument, featuring **GEORGE WASHINGTON** on a horse, was commissioned in 1857 and unveiled in 1869. The famous *MAKE WAY FOR DUCKLINGS* SCULPTURE, presented in 1987, is based on the 1941 bestselling picture book of the same name.

CAN YOU FIND...

NOW THAT YOU'RE HERE, WOULD YOU MIND HELPING ME FIND A FEW OTHER ITEMS?

x2

THE NEW ENGLAND AQUARIUM

THE NEW ENGLAND AQUARIUM opened in 1969 as the first private, nonprofit aquarium in the city and had the goal of creating an underwater experience that would connect the city to the waterfront. In 1970, the **GIANT OCEAN TANK** exhibit opened, which was then the world's largest circular saltwater tank. The aquarium has been active in rescuing stranded marine mammals and helping to protect the endangered **NORTH ATLANTIC RIGHT WHALE**.

Today, the aquarium has thousands of marine animals, a four-story coral reef, and the largest shark and ray touch tank on the East Coast. Over **1.3 MILLION VISITORS** come each year to see penguins, sea lions, octopuses, whales, sea turtles, various fish, and more! There are also meet-and-greet sessions with harbor seals and **MYRTLE THE GREEN SEA TURTLE**, who first joined the tank in 1970.

CAN YOU FIND...

$8.99

FANEUIL HALL

FANEUIL HALL was built in 1742 as a gift to the city of Boston from merchant **PETER FANEUIL**. It was originally used as a central marketplace for crops and livestock but was nicknamed **"THE CRADLE OF LIBERTY"** when it became a platform for the country's most famous orators such as Samuel Adams and George Washington. In 1826, Faneuil Hall expanded to include **QUINCY MARKET**. In the 1970s, the marketplace was renovated and reopened with a fresh name—**FANEUIL HALL MARKETPLACE**.

Today, more than **18 MILLION** people visit the marketplace each year to experience the shops, restaurants, and outdoor entertainment. Visitors can also enjoy **STREET PERFORMANCES** like stunts, balance routines, music, and more, which have been a part of Faneuil Hall's entertainment since the 1970s when performers began entertaining construction workers.

CAN YOU FIND...

WHILE YOU'RE HERE, CAN YOU ALSO FIND THESE OBJECTS?

CARSON BEACH

CARSON BEACH is part of a three-mile stretch of parks and beaches along the SOUTH BOSTON SHORELINE. This sandy beach, owned and maintained by the Commonwealth's Department of Conservation and Recreation, is popular for swimming and has a great view of BOSTON HARBOR. There are walkways, benches, shade shelters, volleyball courts, and award-winning landscaping. The recently renovated EDWARD J. MCCORMACK BATHHOUSE has restrooms, changing rooms, showers, drinking water fountains, chess tables, and bocce courts.

In addition to swimming, visitors to the beach can bike, walk, fish, picnic, or simply enjoy the sun and the view. The newly-renovated "MOTHER'S REST" is a picnic area with a fishing pier nearby.

CAN YOU FIND...

BOSTON LOGAN INTERNATIONAL AIRPORT

The **BOSTON LOGAN INTERNATIONAL AIRPORT** was dedicated on September 8, 1923. Originally called Jeffrey Field, the airfield was used by the Massachusetts **AIR GUARD** and the **ARMY AIR CORPS**, but commercial flights began a few years later. In 1943, the airport was officially renamed the **GENERAL EDWARD LAWRENCE LOGAN INTERNATIONAL AIRPORT** in honor of a local war hero.

The airport is one of the nation's busiest, serving tens of millions of passengers each year across forty airlines. Surrounded by Boston Harbor on three sides, the airport is limited to its **1,700-ACRE SIZE**. Visitors can enjoy restaurants, shops, and art exhibits from local artists and institutions, as well as a 9/11 memorial, "a place of reflection and remembrance for all those affected by the events of **SEPTEMBER 11, 2001**."

CAN YOU FIND...

← GATES ✈

AIRPORT JAVA CAFE

CHECK-IN 0-55

FRANKLIN PARK ZOO

Founded in 1912, the **FRANKLIN PARK ZOO** is a 72-acre site tucked in a historic Boston neighborhood. On its opening day, 10,000 visitors came to see the zoo's first exhibit with bears from Germany and Yellowstone National Park. Despite early success, the zoo struggled during the Great Depression and WWII and fell into disrepair. Throughout the 1980s, the **FRANKLIN PARK COALITION** worked to revitalize the zoo, and by 1990, it became accredited.

Visitors today can see birds, giraffes, zebras, lions, kangaroos, warthogs, tigers, hippopotamuses, giant anteaters, reptiles, and much more. The **FRANKLIN FARM** exhibit provides a glimpse at farm life, and the **CHILDREN'S ZOO** gives visitors an opportunity to interact with wildlife. Zookeeper chats are available in Bird's World, Franklin Farm, and the Tropical Forest—where visitors can also watch gorillas being fed!

CAN YOU FIND...

THANK YOU FOR FINDING THESE ITEMS ACROSS THIS GREAT CITY. NOW OUR BOSTON EXHIBIT IS GOING TO BE A HIT, ALL THANKS TO YOU!

IF YOU'RE UP FOR AN EXTRA CHALLENGE, CAN YOU GO BACK AND FIND THESE OTHER HIDDEN ITEMS IN EACH SCENE?